THE EVE EFFECT, "SECRETS TO GETTING YOUR DESIRED RESULTS FROM HIM"

By

ANTHONY L. WILSON

ISBN-13: 978-0988298750

ISBN-10: 0988298759

Foreword

I am honored to speak on my friend, Pastor Anthony Wilson. When I think of Pastor Wilson, the word "leader" instantly comes to mind. He is and has been a leader since our days in the classroom. As a former military officer, I have had the wonderful opportunity to see many young people turn into mighty leaders. It is safe to say, that Pastor Wilson has been a leader since the 3rd grade.

Since I have known him, Pastor Wilson has had God's light shining on him and it has transpired through him into the pulpit and to his family and friends. Even in school, other children would listen with a tentative ear as he directed and led. Several teachers dotted on him because he was very respectful, a calm and caring soul. To this day, his demeanor holds the same, so it's befitting that he write a book on respectful relationships.

The Eve Effect is a book that celebrates and challenges women. It gives us the praise we most deserve, however it makes us aware. Aware of our effect on our men. Pastor Wilson breaths life into this book with serious under-tones mixed with tongue and cheek laughter. In the end, those who read this book may have a new awareness of their relationships both in dating and marriage.

Again, Pastor Wilson is and has been for years a leader in our communities. His sermons have touched people from all over the world. His book, the Eve Effect will do the same.

Raquel Riley Thomas

U.S. Army Veteran (Ordnance Officer)

Mrs. America 1st Runner-Up (2010-11)

Dr. Maya Angelou is quoted as saying "when you know better, you do better". In an age when marriage is becoming more of an option rather than a necessity and divorces, both of believers and non-believers are starting to be equal, discussions need to take place about the breakdown of relationships and marriages. While we all know someone who has experienced a breakdown of a relationship, the infamous question is always "what happened". More and more women are stating it is difficult to enter into and/or maintain a relationship. The question is, is it more difficult or is it most people do not have the right tools in order to maintain an effective and long term relationship?

The Eve Effect by Anthony Wilson is a relationship tool for those desiring relationships, those in relationships and those coming out of a relationship wanting better relationships in the future. According to an article in Forbes Magazine, in 2008, 74% of self-help books on love and relationships were purchased by women. Women are staying single longer, marrying later and it is in part due to what they feel is the inability to have a quality relationship which leads to marriage. While it is easy to blame the problem on our male counterparts, it may not be the only answer to the problem. Another answer may be we are in need of practical, real-life information to help us successfully be in relationship with our male counterparts.

The old cliché tells us if you want to know the truth you have to go straight to the horse's mouth. In other words, for the truth, go straight to the source. If we want to know how to have a relationship with a man, we have to know how the man thinks, feels and operates. Pastor Wilson has taken the time to give us a first-hand view into the psychology of men. In a raw and straight to the point manner, Pastor Wilson explains the male ego and the power women have to energize or alienate the man in their lives with their words and actions.

One of the most powerful effects of this book, making it stand out from some others, is the ability to diffuse and disavow the concept of women manipulating men to get what they want. Pastor Wilson, by explaining the male psyche, teaches and equips women to empower the man in their lives by honest demonstration of the tools presented. The information provided by Pastor Wilson helps women learn to work with their men towards a strong and fulfilling relationship rather than working against him causing him to mentally, emotionally and eventually physically withdraw from the relationship.

It is my prayer, as a pastor and a life coach, women and men will be empowered through this book. It is my hope women will be equipped with practical tools to help them identify and connect with the men in their lives. Men will feel empowered to allow the women in their lives to have access to them not only physically but emotionally, mentally and spiritually in order to build a healthier union. It is my hope through this book; real dialogue will begin to happen between men and women to help change the trajectory of relationships in our society in which we move away from long-term singleness and high divorce rates to healthy courtships leading to healthy, long-lasting relationships.

Pastor Evita L. Smith, M.Div.
Kingdom Seekers Community Church
Next Chapter Coaching, Inc.

Acknowledgements.....

I am sincerely grateful for the opportunity of being in a position to be a blessing to so many lives on a consistent and regular basis. In that, I am well aware of the fact that others have been a blessing to me as well.

I want to take this moment to acknowledge those individuals who are directly responsible for inspiring and motivating me to get to this point in my life: *To my family, My sons, Anthony Jr (Tj), Myles and Nigil, to my Mother Alma, Father John, Sisters Tonia and Sheyna and my only Big Brother Randy, and awesome Niece Jaala. To my uncle Fred and Aunt Janice. My friends, Shelby, Ken, Melanie Nicole, Nez, Los, Hamner, Oliver, Stokes, Angela S., M.Davis, C.T, My church family CHURCH180*

Did you hear about.......?

There was a prominent Mayor and his lovely wife who left the Mayor's Ball one evening to go home for the night. On the way, the Mayor decided to stop and get gas to put into their Mercedes Benz. As they pulled up, the gas attendant came to the car and asked, "How may I help you?" The Mayor politely said to him, "Fill it up, please." The gas attendant filled up the car, the Mayor handed one hundred dollars to the attendant. The gas came to sixty- five dollars and the other thirty five was a tip to the attendant. The attendant gratefully told the Mayor, "Thank you kindly sir." The Mayor said,

"You're welcome" and begins to drive off. However, when they reached the traffic light, the Mayor said to his wife, "Did you recognize who that guy was? He was your old boyfriend from high school." She said, "Yes I knew who he was!" The Mayor went on to say, "Aren't you glad you married me, the prominent Mayor of this great city?" The wife responded, "Yes I am glad and proud to be married to you! But if I had married him, he would be the prominent Mayor and you would have been pumping gas!" - THE EVE EFFECT

The Guide

Introduction/Why this book

Chapter 1   Pg. 21
Size Does Matter (how you handle it, could mean everything)

Chapter 2   Pg. 61
Behind Curtain Number 1, 2 or 3 (three types of men you will meet)

Chapter 3   Pg. 83
You'd Be Surprised To Know (misunderstandings and myths about men)

Chapter 4   Pg. 105
Use Your P; Get Results (traits every woman have to possess and perform)

Chapter 5   Pg. 121
Be A Facilitator, Not A Manipulator (there's actually a thin line you should not cross)

Chapter 6   **Pg. 135**
18 Seconds (are you sure you want to make this compromise?)

Chapter 7   **Pg. 145**
Listen, Listen, Listen (did you hear what you think you heard?)

Chapter 8   **Pg. 159**
Please Don't (things you may not want to do)

Chapter 9   **Pg.177**
Your Secret Weapon (I saved the best for last...you can thank me later)

Introduction/Why This Book?

So there's much talk as of late of what it takes

to have a vibrant, stable and long lasting

relationship these days. It is the hottest topic

trending on social media, in break rooms, at the

gyms and around some dining table somewhere.

Most are consumed with finding the "right one!"

This is especially frustrating to women who, from

childhood age, have always wanted her knight in

shining armor to come and sweep her off her feet.

Only to discover that in real life, it is hard to have

that fantasy, UNTIL NOW!!!

For you see, some asked me in the planning

stages of this book, why this type of book in a

seemingly saturated sea of all the others out on the

market. My reply was simple. WHY NOT ONE

MORE? Because, at the end of the day, just as

people are different, many times, people receive

information differently and even more so, another

different perspective can only help and not hurt

anyone. However, that's not the primary reason

for this book.

As we look closely at our culture, the family

dynamic is being challenged to maintain its

purpose for which it was made. In other words,

longevity in marriages are pretty much a non factor

and instant satisfaction is at the top of the menu

today!! Thus, comes the finger pointing as to who

is the blame for all of this. The women are

blaming the men, men blaming the women. The

men and the women together are blaming the

media and the media is blaming people for their

inability to separate entertainment from reality.

My opinion is that everyone involved in your

relationship is the blame. It's called being human!

We make mistakes, we make decisions that are

based upon our feelings, our experiences, our

imaginations and the list goes on. But I want to

introduce to you something that could very well

solve all of your relationship woes. It's called THE

EVE EFFECT.

The say what? Yes, you heard correctly, THE

EVE EFFECT! Oh, I can actually read your mind

right about now. You are asking what is THE

EVE EFFECT? Well before I answer that question,

I must explain where this concept comes from. It

comes from a story, that for some, a mythological one in nature and for others the core of their religious beliefs. Nonetheless, a story about a man by the name of Adam who was specifically told by his creator not to eat of a tree that was located in the middle of a garden called Eden. Adam's creator told him not to partake of the tree's fruit. That seem like a simple order, but His creator also explained to him, the consequences for disobeying him would be that of death. All was well, until his wife, who was easily influenced by a serpent (yes a serpent) to indulge in the very thing her husband was prohibited from eating. Still, up to this point all was well. Adam had not eaten of the tree. However, his wife Eve did.

It was in one brief moment, of nothing short of the most powerful pivotal point of all time, Eve gave what was forbidden to her husband Adam. There was something about that woman Eve, whereby Adam could not resist what she offered. Adam took it and ate what his creator explicitly told him not to. Ok, maybe you missed what I just said! Adam was willing to risk the loss of Paradise and even die for what Eve was offering to him. It was an 'effect' that no one or nothing can deny existed. What is interesting about this 'effect' of Eve having on Adam back then, is that if you look closely at our world today, it is still in effect! Women, just like Eve, have the ability to get the same results she received back in the Garden of Eden. She desired her husband Adam to receive and partake of what she wanted him to have. Eve,

without nagging, coercing, without complaining,

without crying, without throwing things, just

simply had a desire, conveyed it and Adam

willingly participated with NO objections.

Therefore, this simple, yet profound gesture of

handing a piece of fruit to her husband, Adam, has

made all the difference in the world for

relationships since that epic act.

In the following chapters, I want to inform

many and remind others of what (every), and I

repeat (every) woman has in her possession right

now. It's called THE EVE EFFECT. So, what

exactly is THE EVE EFFECT? At best, it can be

described as the undeniable, unexplainable,

irresistible influence that women have on men. It's

that thing that at the end of every movie that will

have the hero to go back into the most dangerous

situation to rescue some damsel in distress. It is

that thing that will make a singer write a number

one hit song. It is that thing that will make a

painter create the most historic and valuable

portrait of all time. It is that thing that will make a

construction worker read a recipe book, take salsa

lessons, and write poetry so he can orchestrate the

perfect date. It is that very thing that will cause a

thug to drop the "t" and be the most affectionate

guy he can be to his woman. What is this thing, it

is THE EVE EFFECT. In short it is

IRRESISTABLE INFLUENCE on a man.

However, having THE EVE EFFECT is one thing,

but knowing what to do with it, is something altogether different.

The frustration for most women is that, they aren't getting what they desire and need from men. What if I could ease many, if not most, of your frustrations? What if I could empower you with information that will revolutionize how you date and interact with men to the point he can't resist the honor and opportunity of "putting a ring on it?" I want to share with you *secrets to getting your desired results from him*..... So, if you need a clear cut definition of what THE EVE EFFECT is, it can be defined as the God given intuitive influence that a woman has over a man. However, this book is about empowering you with inside information that will allow you the ability to better relate to men. So get into a place of solitude for the next

few days and pay real close attention to one of the

most powerful books you will ever read.

CHAPTER 1 – *SIZE DOES MATTER*

(How you handle it, could mean everything)

Already I see the smile on your face! I can hear your thoughts saying, "I know that's right." However, this chapter has nothing to do with what you are smiling about or thinking about. A real woman recognizes that the male anatomy will not guarantee anything that is meaningful and long lasting. So what is this idea of 'SIZE DOES MATTER?' Well it is the largest thing on every man. It is so huge that it impacts everything about the man. It is so gigantic that if you are not careful, you could trip over it! Uh oh, what could be so big? It's called the male ego.

THE FOUNDATION OF HIS EGO

This chapter is going to explain to you that how

you handle this huge piece of a man's reality,

could mean success or failure in your relationship.

It could mean your marriage lasting five months or

fifty-five years. So, what is the Ego? A simple

definition of what the ego is; it is a person's sense

of self esteem or self-importance. It can extend to

the feeling of one's pride and their perceived

superiority over others. It is how one personally

perceives themselves. However, when it comes to

men, there are some unique aspects about the male

ego that women need to know. First of all,

research has shown that the development of the

male ego comes from a son's relationship with his

mother. She is the first woman that he encounters

in life. Therefore the son soon does all he can to make his mother proud of him. She in return responds back to him with the highest admiration, celebration and affirmation that often develops his sense of worth and value. Just think of some of the things you hear mothers say to their sons when they are small. From such statements like, "you are such a big boy!", "you go boy!", "you are one handsome young man!" and a simple, "I'm so proud of you!" is all the fuel needed to help develop the ego and self esteem of a male child. So when boys grow into adulthood, it is not surprising that men place so much value in the opinions of their significant other, or the one they pledge the rest of their life with. Women must get this down into the depths of their beings and that is we, as men, are doing everything to please a

woman, somewhere and somehow. From, the car

we drive to the clothes we wear, we have you in

mind. From the house we purchase or place to stay

to the amount of money we have, we have you in

mind. Think about it for a moment…. If we think

that you think that what we have, wear, or even our

conversation is lame or boring to you, we will

make whatever adjustments we have too, because

you help boost our egos, thus we internalize your

response to us and it helps shape the continued

'self-importance' we need. We "unspokenly" need

to know that the woman in our lives, hold us in the

highest regard. Let me be one of the first to repeat

again that 'stroking our egos' is one of the most

single important roles you play in a relationship

with your husband or boyfriend. Now what I can not tell you is what it takes to 'stroke' your particular man's ego. But whatever it is, you must be willing to do it. HOWEVER ladies, what I am about to explain to you, is the most classified piece of information you will ever get, that you may not have thought of and that is....., though our egos are big, our egos are sooooooo delicate! This is why 'The Eve Effect' is so critical. (You are going to hear that word critical a lot) You have to know how, in your own way, to keep the largest yet most delicate and fragile thing of a man, properly maintained. I am going to give a few suggestions in a minute, but let's go deeper into this thought.

The man's ego is so intrinsically tied to the words of the woman, because remember, the first person that ever boosted and developed his ego

was his mother who, consequently, is a woman.

Just think about it! A grown man standing 6'3 and

220 pounds will score a touchdown and have all

the world watching him front and center in a

camera and the first person he wants to

acknowledge is his first "ego stroker," his mother!

This is why, for some of you reading this book,

have made that phone call or visited 'HER' (THE

MOTHER) because you noticed at some point that

she still has a major influence in his life. Can I tell

you why? The reason is that in the eyes of mama,

'her boy can do no wrong!' Now, although, we

know this is not true but there's a wonderful

principle here you must see. That is, if we as men

are influenced by the words that come out of the

mouth of the woman we love, honor and respect. It

is most often, his mother who comes first until you

become his 'new' woman to exchange positions

with mom, as the continued builder of his ego. I

know you are probably thinking that this is too

much to do for your husband, your boyfriend, or

your significant other. You can't live up to nor

will you try to take the place of his mother. That is

exactly not what I am saying. You can't do

anything until you have his time, his attention, his

heart and the rest will follow. You are not in

competition with his mother as far as he is

concerned. As a side note, there are some mothers

who will not let their sons 'leave' and 'cleave' to

the woman of his dreams. (Now, that's another

book!). However, once he gives you his heart, it

will be imperative that you know what to do and what not to do with his ego.

THE EGO FACTOR

Well consider this.... If all of his efforts are to ultimately please and win your approval (and it is), yet he feels he can not gain or win your approval, then the search is on to fill the void of having his ego massaged or stroked. The results of this can and sometimes will go as far as a complete disconnect with you emotionally and mentally, yet not necessarily physically. Which means, mentally your mate can check out of the relationship THE MOMENT his ego is damaged by you. Keep in your mind at all times, and I do mean ALL TIMES, your man wants to please you. He needs validation from you. Most women never really

take this seriously because they feel that we should

just "man up" when it comes to our emotions and

feelings. Well guess what ladies, we "man up" all

the time; on our jobs we "man up," in the streets

we "man up," and always around our male

counterparts, we have to "man up!" However,

ladies you are not the job, you are not the streets or

even another man. You are his Queen, his woman,

his boo, his breath, his reason for living, often

times his 'latest and greatest inspiration!' But

when you mishandle his ego that man can and very

well, will check out mentally and emotionally yet

he is able to fulfill many of the physical aspects of

the relationship. Now hear this closely again! He

can continue to carry on the normal physical

aspects of the relationship with the inclusion of

being there to pay the bills, be there for the kid's

games, for the family outings and so forth.

Because men have been taught, trained and

socialized to discount and hide feelings and

emotions. So, can I tell you what is happening all

this time after 'ego damage?' He is actually

waiting for his body to catch up with his already

absent emotions and mind. He will exit the

relationship or marriage without a formal notice, a

note, an email, or even a text. He has the capacity

to just leave without warning or explanation. And

so many women have come to me to saying I

didn't see this coming. He was still sleeping with

me. He was still going on vacations with the

family. He was still paying the bills. And

seemingly out of no where, he just up and leaves.

No ladies, he left some time before emotionally,

mentally and what you are seeing in his recent

departure is that his body has finally caught up

with everything else that has left prior. Listen

carefully, for the sake of respect and a sense of self

worth and a desire to be needed, a man will go to

great lengths to protect his ego. I am not talking

about right or wrong here, but I am just talking

about reality. Because, most often, we have been

the most vulnerable with you. We have entrusted

with you, our fears and phobias. And when you

damage our egos with the words and actions you

relay to us, it ultimately says that we can not trust

you because we feel you will use those things, you

know about us, against us. We may often think, if

you did not know as much as you had, you could

not and would not say what you may have said or

done. In other words, we connect all of your

words and actions back to the most sensitive

information we shared with you during our dating

or marriage. And sometimes, not all the time,

there is no recovery from a man being 'ego

damaged' by the woman he loves. You must know

that, we as men, we hear in general terms. We

often are only interested in the big picture most

often and not the specific details that most women

are. It's critical (there's that word again) that you

clearly understand this principle. Let's say for

instance, your husband or boyfriend does

something that has you pretty upset. And you tell

him, you are so "irresponsible" or you can't do

anything right. He will often only hear the word

"irresponsible" and attach that word to the general

expression of how you feel about him on

everything. That word that you used as his

woman, now says that all the other responsible

things he HAS done have been overshadowed by

one mistake or a few mistakes he has made. So

now his ego is damaged because he no longer sees

himself in her eyes as 'The Man' but some

irresponsible dude that she is tolerating. He will

possibly go into defense mode and you now

become his enemy and not his energy for doing his

best! Let me say it this way, you don't want to go

from being his energy to becoming his enemy

because of what, how and when you say hurtful

things to him. How can you avoid some of these pitfalls? It's called The Eve Effect.

FEED THAT THANG

You have within you the ability to be an impact and influence on that man more that you can ever know. I shared with you earlier that I am going to show you how to maintain this huge yet delicate thing called the male ego. Ok, you have two tools in your possession when it comes to boosting our egos and nurturing the delicacy of that same ego. They, are of course, your words and your actions. Your words of affirmation go a long way with us. We love compliments. We love it when you brag on us! We love when you send random messages about what we do to you! We love even when you tell us how guys try to get your attention but you

let them know they don't have a chance in "h..."

because we are your king. Ok, I hear some of you!

You are saying, I can do that and I already do that,

but it seems to not be working. Now you have to

pull out your second tool; your actions! Your

actions have communication capabilities, too. For

example, when at gatherings, make his plate of

food while he sits down and serve him with a smile

on your face. When possible, make him look good

in front of his friends by showing them that "He's

In Charge" of your home (of course we all know

who is in charge).

Learn to like what he loves. This may mean

you have to learn to like sports. It may mean you

may need to learn the ins and outs of his favorite

team and then spark up a conversation about what

you've learned. If he's into motorcycles, learn the

ins and outs to the motorcycle culture. If he's in a

fraternity, learn to like some of the 'interesting' or

what may appear 'boring' things that they do.

Even if he is into video games, learn what his

favorite game is and try to play it with him. Why

should you do these things? Simple, they are

important to him along with the fact that you are to

him too! Now he doesn't have to feel that you are

in competition with things he likes or things he

loves to do. To have you into what he's into,

makes him feel he now has the 'perfect' girlfriend

or wife. He will brag about you to his friends and

thus it all goes to his ego in a positive way.

Brush up against him in a seductive way to let

him know he is turning you on. Let me hang out

right here for a moment on this thought. One of

the greatest ego boosters in the world is when we

know, that we are turning a woman on. I'm going

to speak to married women now but to the

unmarried women in a later chapter called "18

seconds." Married ladies, when you show us that

we are turning you on, that does something to us.

So, however you do that, do it. Whatever your

threshold of comfort is in your marriage of

'showing' that you are turned on is, do that. In

layman's terms....PUT IT ON HIM! Leave 'sexy'

notes for him where he can see them. Because it

says to us, you can't get enough of us. It let's us

know that we are 'The Man!' I can not really

express in words how we feel when you makes us

feel we are 'handling' that thang and you're loving

it. Men are extremely visual so capitalize on that

fact. Hint, hint! All of this is feeding his ego

which motivates most, if not all, of his actions

concerning you! It can cause him to reach beyond

the norm, push through mediocrity and inspire him

to turn his dreams into realities. You as a woman

have the 'THE EVE EFFECT!' He will respond to

the positive affirmations both verbally and

physically. You have to be his home field

advantage, his 5 star cheerleader, and his 'spinach'

(And you see who Popeye was trying to please.

Olive Oyl), be his personal nurse by bandaging

whatever wounds he may have due to the pressures

of being a man and send him back out to battle.

He will go with pleasure and a sense of pride

because he has you. (In a future chapter, I will

layout for you, in detail, how your Eve Effect

plays a part in all of this)

EGO DAMAGE

I mentioned earlier that if a man feels as though

he fails at pleasing you and you automatically

respond in a negative way, know that it will cause

him to seek something or someone to make him

feel valuable. I know people should never depend

on others to make them feel worth or value. Yet,

people do! Depending on the personality of your

mate, he may communicate his concerns with you,

with you! I hope you caught that. But out of a

desire for peace and no conflict, a lot of men won't

say anything. Why, you may ask? We don't want

to ever appear hurt or weak to you. We don't want

to let you know that you are pushing our buttons.

But on the inside of us, we are in pain, and

frustrated so we cover it up with the negative side

of pride for which is now feeding our ego instead

of your affirmations. You have to know that there

is a positive side of pride in your mate and a

negative side of pride for which the ego thrives on.

I hope you are getting this. If you are feeding our

egos, it builds a sense of positive pride and

appreciation. But when the ego is damaged, the

negative side of pride is activated for which it

won't allow us to express that we are feeling hurt

or unappreciated. So be clear, what you say does

matter because we have given unto you the most of

our prized possession which is our heart. And what a damaged ego means to a man is that he feels he is no longer needed or wanted although those exact words never came out of the woman's mouth.

I want to share with you, from a 2010 CNN report, some things you can do unintentionally that can damage a man's ego; 1. **Making reference to his weight, especially his stomach.** For most men, the stomach is the most visible and repulsive parts of his body in his mind. It will cause him to feel self-conscious and less confident. In addition, defense mode is now up because in our minds that means you are no longer attracted to us. The other side of that is you have to be prepared for retaliatory comments about you. Here is the difference. You won't know the gravity of your words to him because most men hide visible expressions of their emotions.

2. *Being negative about his job*. Even if he downplays his job, he's probably not proud of his work. However, if you say something negative about his work, he will probably feel like you are mocking him. 3. *Comparing him to another man*. This is a major one. The last thing your mate wants to feel is that ANOTHER MAN has your attention. It does not matter who that man is. It can be your father, his father, a brother, uncle, friend of the family, someone on T.V or even your Pastor. In addition, no man wants to feel he is in competition for his woman's affection. Because, that's how we see it when you are really innocent

of not trying to hurt his feelings. 4.

Complimenting some one he dislikes. Because

lots of guys can be vindictive and a simple

compliment directed towards his "enemy" could

prove to be a stab into his ego and that will prove

to be trouble like no other.

5. **Making a negative comment about your**

sessions of intimacy. This could be the

granddaddy of them all. Find a creative way to

speak on what you didn't like, after you talked

about everything you did like. Men equate a great

deal of their entire ability of being a man, to the

bedroom. Come on, repeat that with me again....

'Men equate a great deal of their entire ability of

being a man, to the bedroom.' Don't ask me why!

Just kidding! It is because our egos says so! So

handle with care. I will speak to this subject later

and it is going to drop your jaw. 6. *__Loud talking__*

__him in front of other people.__ Running a close

second to the last ego damager, is being publicly

disrespectful to him by verbally ranting out loud to

him. You have to know when, where and how to

pick and have your battles. Going off in public

with him will definitely cause him to check out the

relationship mentally and emotionally

immediately. 7. *__Criticizing or downplaying his__*

__achievements.__ Whenever he comes to you about

something he has achieved, even if it's small, your

response is of critical importance to him. Your

boost of confidence in him lets him know you are

proud of him and proud of being with him. It is

nothing, absolutely nothing, like hearing the

woman he loves say I'm proud of being with you.

He will work even harder at whatever he is doing

to make a living, make a vision come to pass or

just making himself a better person. But the

opposite is just as horrific for him. To hear that

she is ashamed of his efforts and ashamed of being

with him will produce wounds that no top surgeon

could repair. In short, when you damage a man's

ego intentionally or unintentionally, you must see

yourself as someone who has seasoned and

tenderized raw meat for a 'PRIDE!' In other

words, a pack of lioness are called a 'Pride.' You

know the old cliché. One person's trash is another

person's treasure.

EGO RECOVERY

Here you are! You've been introduced to the

biggest thing a man possesses that has only three

letters, E-G-O. I have shared with you the

foundation of the ego, the ego factor, feeding the

ego, ego damage and now I want to enlighten you

on EGO RECOVERY. The belief has been that

once a man's ego is damaged, bruised or hurt, that

there's no returning back to normal. Well again,

let's look at what is tied to the ego of a man. It is

the man's desire to please his woman. The man's

self esteem and self importance is always tied to

that desire. His sense of pride and respect are

wrapped up in his ego, as well. And when all of

that is damaged, one can be justified in saying that

there is no way his ego can return to normal. Well

it is safe to say that it all depends. If you are

married, then your concern would be if your

husband has had his ego damaged by you, is he

trying to, has, or is seeking something or someone

to stroke his ego? My answer is, it depends. If you

are dating someone, you are probably wondering if

your boyfriend has had his ego damaged by you, is

he trying to, has or is seeking someone or

something to stroke his ego. My answer is simply,

it depends! It depends on what kind of man you

are with in your marriage or dating. It will depend

on what he values the most. It will depend on his

ability to forgive and heal. It will depend on the

depth of his love, devotion and commitment he has

for you. I do believe that a man can stay faithful

and true to his wife or mate even when his ego has

been damaged. However, women you must allow him time to be your friend while he is in ego recovery mode. Like I said before, you may feel this is just over the top and no real man will be all so sensitive like that. That the man should just 'man up' forgive you and keep it moving even if you hurt his 'little' feelings. Well if you feel that way, you underestimate men. Again, a damaged ego doesn't mean he won't sleep with you, pay bills, or take care of home! A damaged ego means his body is there with you but his mind is on Delta, AirTran, Southwest or on the other side of town. A damaged ego means you could wake up one day and your husband or mate is gone with no forwarding address. But if you allow his ego to recover from being damaged by you, his recovery could help restore some trust in you and not cause

resentment. This will require your apology

verbally and your actions to be consistent. If your

husband or mate is in ego recovery mode, your

words from here on out will be significant.

Consider how you speak to him. Speaking to him

with positive and reassuring words will help treat

the wounded area. I'm not implying you be

subservient in the relationship, but what I am

suggesting is that you be smart. Sincerely care

about his needs for awhile. Because once he feels

that you care, with not only words, but with

actions, he will be more open to sharing with you

again those things that are important to him.

That's your goal! Having him to open back up to

you. Let me tell you why. Most of the time,

initially, men don't have anyone to talk to about

their problems. I'm talking about those heart

wrenching problems. But at some point, someone

or something will pique his interest to open up to

and the last person you, as his woman or wife,

want is it to be another woman. Because there are

some women who will love to have your husband

or boyfriend. And sometimes, we, as men, don't

come with ego stroking filters. If we are hurt,

because we can't really express our emotions, will

be susceptible to those women lying in wait for

your emotionally wounded mate. Now, I can hear

you thinking again. No, I am in no way excusing a

man for being unfaithful to you. The correct thing

to do is for him to come to you and end the

relationship with you before he participates in

another relationship. But this part of the book is

not about right or wrong. It is about knowing how

men tick. How we respond to situations brought

upon on by our egos being damaged. However, if

we decide to stay, we are saying that we are

willing to put our egos into recovery and try to get

to a place where we can move on. I can't

guarantee that things will get back to where they

were before the ego damage, but you can start

from where you are and move on to a healthy

relationship. It all begins with not only you saying

you are sorry, but also showing him, too.

Many women underestimate the power of their

actions towards us. As you already know, men are

extremely visual and physical creatures. So the

touchy feely stuff registers so much quicker than

the verbal affirmations. In other words, we love

when you say certain things to us. We don't

negate the words, however, when you put actions

with those words, now you are really speaking our

language. Yes this is a general rule, because there

are some men, who only want physical touching

for sexual satisfaction. But for the most part, most

men are extremely accepting of continual moments

of being rubbed, caressed or kissed on. I dare you

to try this one day. If your mate's ego has been

damaged, you now recognize that he is in ego

recovery mode, one of the best ways to let him

know you are sorry and want things restored, tell

him that you are going to give him a king for

weekend experience. Now of course, if you don't

want things better, him better, your relationship

better, go ahead and go to the next chapter.

However, if you took your vows seriously and

your commitment seriously, a king for a weekend

experience will get things headed back in the right

direction quickly. Now if he is willing to accept

your offer, I'm almost pretty sure, he will not only

forgive you, but the pain associated with his ego

being damage, may go away. Because we are

physical, visual and action oriented creatures.

Here are some suggestions for King for weekend

experience:

1. *Tell him he doesn't have to do anything for*
the weekend accept enjoy himself. Now,

depending on where he is emotionally, that will be

some of the best news ever. For him to feel that

it's all about him, will put a super smile in his

heart although he may not want to show it on his

face. So don't be alarmed if his initial response

isn't what you expected. Remember and keep

focus of the task at hand. Keep in mind and try to

see yourself in his shoes during this critical

moment. Because, as I stated earlier, if his ego is

damaged and you are unsuspecting of the fact that

his 'heart or emotions' have already left the

premises, get ready for your Little House on the

Prairie to become a Nightmare on Elm street. So

like I said, his initial response may seem to be

nonchalant, but trust me, he is smiling on the

inside. However, if he refuses your offer, then

chances are, ego recovery may not be his solution.

In his mind, it over. But let's just say ego recovery

is where he is. Which means yes he is hurt, but he

is willing to work through the pain and move on

the next chapter of your union. Let him know that

for the next 48 hours, it's going to be all about

him. I'm getting excited now for him! Because,

really what you are letting him know is that most

men don't get this kind of treatment. He probably

can't come up with an instance where his buddies

told him, that their wives or girlfriends gave them

a similar experience for which he is about to have.

So make a big to do about giving him King for

Weekend experience.

2. *Tell him to give you a list of everything that he*

would want to do or have done to him that

weekend. This gives you an idea of what to do and

allow you a chance to plan. Now be prepared

mentally for whatever he puts down. At this point,

I can't really predetermine what your husband or

boyfriend desires. We are all different when it

comes to some things. But let me list a few

possibilities. He may want to watch sports all day

and all night. If so, provide him with the

necessities of his favorite food and beverages that

makes his sport watching fun. He may want

breakfast in bed or all his meals in bed. He may

desire to get a massage from either you or a

professional. The key is whatever he needs to feel

like he is the most important thing to you those 48

hours. The attention he is getting will help to put

him at ease about recent events that may have been

damaging for him. Now of course, if he says

something that is beyond your scope of executing,

just say, I may not can do it now, but hopefully

one day I can. If you have kids, find a way to

work it out where they are either not there or that

they are informed of what you expect from them

that weekend. Ladies, do what you have to do to

make this happen.

3. *Let it be known to your friends and his, you*

enjoyed treating him like a king! Now at this

point, I must reiterate something I have said and

that is, it was words that pushes him into ego

damage mode but it is going to take a combination

of words and work to allow him to recover. No

one has to know why you did what you did. He

just need to know that you took so much pleasure

in doing so, that you had to tell someone else. See

to it to have his friends know that you treated him

like a king and that you enjoyed it, does a couple

of things for you. First of all, it is a major ego

boost. But secondly, and most importantly, it

places a level of accountability on him. Think

about it if you will. If for whatever reason your

husband or mate tries to bring up the possibility of

him looking somewhere else or doing something

else with someone else in the presence of his

friends, most of the time, those same friends will

remind him that he had better not jeopardize what

he has 'at home.'

I hope you are getting what I am saying. Yes, you

can be pessimistic and say that nothing will stop a

man from doing what they are going to do. That is

true, but it could also mean that you can keep an

eye on him without having your eye on him

through his friends because now they know how

'great' he has it at home! In the mind of your

husband or mate, you have put together a great

therapeutic solution to his ego being damaged and

put him on the road to recovery by not only telling

him that you are sorry for damaging his ego but by

also showing him you are sorry. We listen a bit

more clearly when you do on the same level as you

say. Once he is back to a place of having trust in

you, do all you can to never take him there (ego

damage) again. For you will more than likely end

up with a man that will stay with you for the sake

of convenience and finances, but will never trust

you with his heart because HE WILL give it to

someone or something else. I have seen it so many

times that it all comes out at funerals. In that, a

man can have a completely separate family on the other side of town and it doesn't come to the light until his untimely death. Don't let that be you!

CHAPTER 2 – BEHIND CURTAIN NUMBER
1, 2, or 3
(Three types of men you will meet)

One of my favorite game shows of all time is

the game show, *'Let's make a deal.'* For many of

you who remember this show, it is centered on a

contestant given one opportunity to choose a

particular curtain that veils either a prize or gaffe.

The only information you have about the

possibility of what is behind the curtain is a good

guess and gut instincts. However, that often

proved to not be enough to win a prize. Instead of

going home with a dining room set, car or a dream

vacation, you could very well leave with a million

dollars in Monopoly money. Well the same could

be said in relationships. Often when we initially

meet people, most of the time, all we see is the

curtain. And sometimes, the only information you

have is a good guess and gut instincts about what

is behind that curtain. Because I realize THE EVE

EFFECT in you, I want to give you some

information about what is behind those three

curtains. It comes down to you understanding that

there are only three types of men, you will ever

meet. I want you to listen closely and listen

carefully about what I am about to explain to you.

Some of you are already in a marriage, some of

you are in a committed relationship, some of you

are in the beginning stages of dating someone and

the rest of you desire to be in a relationship. This

means one of two things. You either already know

what kind of person you have or you don't have a

clue. I want to suggest that behind curtain number 1, 2, and 3 you will find your man or a certain type of man.

CURTAIN 1 – THE MAN WITH NO OPTIONS

This guy is every where. You see him out and about. He is at the job, he is at the gym, he is at the local hangout and he is even at the church. You can pretty much spot him from a distance. He lacks 'swag.' He doesn't have that pizzazz. You can only see him as a friend and nothing more however he wants a relationship with you at any cost. He is that guy that is often a good guy, in some regards, or he is overcompensating for many things. He will do anything to get your attention.

He doesn't really come with the kind of conversation that keeps your attention. He is borderline 'lame' but you can see he is a good person, just not for you! If you aren't careful, he could be stalk(ish) because he spends so much time trying to get your approval and attention that you sometimes lean on the side of caution. This man compliments you even when you know you are bumming that day. He thinks you are perfect while at the same time you kind of feel sorry for him. You are always trying to set him up with other people knowing all the while he wants to be with you.

I call this man 'the guy with no options' because he doesn't know how to court a woman. He only sees what he likes and doesn't know how to get it even if you paid him. He could be this way because of his lack of experience with women so he's left to try things he saw on television or in a movie, or what his friends keep telling him to do. This guy is so predictable and often gullible. He is the guy that if you went out on a friendly date, he won't be able to make decisions while on the date. He is all about what you want even if you decided to bring some other friends along with you. This kind of guy just doesn't have what it takes to have you acknowledge him. However, because of your kind heartedness, you may allow him to be around you. You may 'use' him for things when you are out of options yourself. How ironic? Now catch what I am about to say. Add it to the vast array of knowledge you have about men. You can't just say that this kind of guy is lame or just lacks

confidence. You must make the mental note that

he is a man with little to no options. Most, if not

all, women are attracted to men that have genuine

confidence, not cockiness, just authentic

confidence. You can spot a non confident man and

it does not work for you at all and that is

understood. In addition to that, the man with no

options will sometimes be a man that is sweet and

kind for the wrong reasons. They often are trying

to prove a point to themselves. They are seeking a

reciprocated response for the kindness they show

women. Because at the end of the day, this type of

man has to often depend on the attention women

give to them in order to experience some sense of

value or confidence in themselves. This type of

man can be a danger or delight to you as a woman.

The key is properly communicating with him

where he stands with you. Notice what I said. It is

letting him know where he stands with you and not

where you stand with him. If his motives and

intentions are pure, then he will stick and stay

around as a friend who just so happens to be male.

You can not send mixed messages to a man with

no options. Because here's the most critical

element about all this. The man with no options

does not see himself as the man with no options

and most women don't realize he is a man without

options. Yes believe me when I tell you, it doesn't

click in some women's minds that this kind of man

doesn't have any real options. And for now, he

has for some reason, made you a priority. Can I

share with you what some of you have probably

analytically figured out about the man with no

options? He is doing all he can to wait for a weak

moment in your life. Even more so, he feels at

some point you will come to your "senses" and

give him his well-deserved shot to be with you.

That is why he is still hanging around. How do

you rid yourself from a man like this, you may

ask? You must cut all communication for starters.

Secondly, you may need a decoy if you know you

will be at a location where he is present. Lastly, if

all of that doesn't work, put Jesus on him. Share

with him that you have prayed and that he wasn't

the one God showed you that you will be with.

Most men in this situation, do not want to hear

anything about God putting you with someone

else. More than likely, he will leave you alone.

Don't lie, do pray about it.

CURTAIN 2 – THE MAN WITH OPTIONS BUT WRONG MENTALITY

Now here is where it gets pretty interesting. The man with options will have a different approach to dealing with you. This guy has everything the man with no options wants to have. He commands attention when he walks into a room. He walks with a confidence that catches most women's attention. He is assertive when he needs to be with you or with any given situation. He knows how to hold a conversation with you because he is pretty experienced with women. He can lure you in because he knows what to say, how to say it and when to say it.....INITIALLY. Have

you ever heard someone say, that when you first

meet someone, they often send their PR

representative? The man with options but wrong

mentality is one of those people. He comes off as

having just what many women want in their mate.

He is polished with a touch of rough edge. In

other words, he knows how to handle himself with

you and others. You realize he gives you a sense

of security that if something surprisingly happens,

he will protect you. Women, you absolutely love

this kind of man. However, I must repeat, that a

man with options but the wrong mentality will

initially be this way. For him it is a pattern. If you

allow me to go deeper, it is a paradigm. It is

absolutely normal for this kind of man to do the

things that he does. This man feels that women are disposable. His mentality is that it's about having fun at the emotional expense of the women he deals with. This man will surprisingly get married. I must say that my heart goes out to a woman who marries a man like this. Some of you have or are currently married to the man with options but wrong mentality. In other words, he married you and kept his options open the whole time you are married. Often it had nothing to do with you. It had nothing to do with you knowing how to take care of him, or doing all your wifely duties. It was his mentality. Men with options but wrong mentalities will take a 'HALF TIME BREAK!' What is a 'half time break?' It is a point in a game where the players take a moment to stop playing, regroup, re-strategize, and refresh themselves in order to get back into 'the game.' So since this kind of man is stuck in this pattern of thinking, some women end up marrying him during 'half time.' Yep this is an issue for many women. Some women have married a man with options but the wrong mentality during his 'half time.' This is a problem because many who married this type of man at the time they did, was under the impression that they were his 'only priority' only to find out later they were just 'one of many options.' Yes ladies he married you in front of the preacher, your family, friends, co-workers and God. And your question is WHY?

Now that tidbit of information was for the married women. It gets just as frustrating for the single women in relationships with men like this.

The most frustrating thing for you is the time and

energy you have put or are putting into the

relationship. Because many women's mindset is to

get married and living happily ever after. The man

with options but wrong mindset is living happy

right now. So, let me tell you how you know you

have become an option in his life. 1. ***How he talks***

to you. If a man that you are in a relationship with

you begins to say hurtful, critical, profane things to

you. YOU ARE JUST AN OPTION! No man

who loves his woman will do such a thing. In fact,

he will at times spare your feelings to the point of

embellishing the truth to do it. Listen, I shared

with you earlier that the foundational centerpiece

of developing a man's ego was his mother. If a

man won't say hurtful, critical and profane things to his mother, he should never and I repeat never say them to you. The moment you are verbally or physically abused, you must not question how he feels about you, now you know it. A real man recognizes who and what you really mean to him. I know some of you have heard that so believe it this time. It is about respect and if a man disrespects you, you have officially been classified as an option to him. Why is this important to know? It means if you decide to leave him, it won't matter!

2. *If you can't locate him*. YOU ARE AN OPTION TO HIM! A man that has you as his priority will go to great lengths to spend time with you. I repeat, great lengths. But the man with

options but the wrong mentality sees himself as the prize and you as a contestant. If you are calling him and he is not picking up the phone or acknowledging you with a text or email. You are an option. Now of course if he communicates where he is before hand, then you have to be mindful and respectful for his inability to respond immediately to you. However, anything outside of that can be an issue. When you are his priority, he wants your time. When you are his priority, he will make time. 3. ***If he doesn't take you anywhere***. YOU ARE AN OPTION TO HIM! When you are a priority to a man, he loves to 'show' you off. He wants other men to know that he has a 'dime' with him. It is a major ego boost for some men just to be with you. But to be with you in public takes that boost off the charts. If he has problems going places with you, chances are he is (a) ashamed of you, or (b) he as other options he doesn't want to mess up with. I cannot pinpoint where or when this type of man got to be like this. I can only speculate and my intent now is to just empower you with information to help you relate to us as men.

CURTAIN 3 – THE MAN WITH OPTIONS AND HAS IT TOGETHER MENTALLY AND SPIRITUALLY

This type of man is often overlooked because of the other type of men you meet. This man is really ideal for most women. He is not perfect but he is close to it. He is authentically concerned about you for the right reasons. He is fully aware of his

strengths and he is consistently working on his

weaknesses because of his relationship with God.

This man has options just like the last man I

introduced you to, except his motives and

intentions are, in his mind, overseen by his God.

Therefore, he is a man of character, a man of

integrity and a man with a good heart. He too,

commands attention when he walks into a room.

He is chivalrous, he is thoughtful and he is a

hopeless romantic. He checks in with you to

provide you with the emotional security every

woman needs. He takes every opportunity to be

with you. He realizes that God said, "It was not

good that he should be alone" and you, in his

mind, are his 'rib.' He is fully aware that the rib is

the strongest bone near the heart to keep it

protected. This type of guy seems wonderful

doesn't he? You are trying to figure out does he

really exist? The answer is Yes! Now there are

other factors that are variable and relevant

depending on a woman's core needs.

Unfortunately, I can't speak on behalf of women

on some subjects. I can with out a doubt, speak for

most men. I said that because, though I have

described to you a seemingly perfect man, I didn't

mention his looks, loot or loving. Those are up to

you as to what is important. I must warn you that

only being preoccupied with a man's exterior can

prove to be the worst decision ever. The other

piece to this is that physical things change but

spiritual and godly things can remain constant.

Therefore, let me show you how to know that you

are possibly being pursued by such a man. First of

all, his conversations will be that of getting to

know you and at the same time revealing himself

to you. He will listen attentively by wanting to

know your vision, goals and desires. He will also

seek to know where God fits into your life. He's

not the "super spiritual" kind of guy, but he will

confidently and caringly have spiritual talks with

you. Secondly, at some point, he will want to

spend time with you at a place of worship. For

him, this is not about running game or playing with

the 'churchy" stuff to get your attention. Because

with or without you, being in worship is a real part

of his life and when he goes to great lengths to

have you a part of that with him, you should count

that as a blessing and not a 'player' move.

Another indicator that you have this type of man,

is he will pray with you and for you.   When you

hear him express himself to God on your behalf,

when it is time to dine, or anytime, you will get a

true sense of his heart and his relationship with

God. In other words, you will know that this isn't

the first time he has had a talk with The Creator.

Lastly, this type of man will be available to you

emotionally. This is crucial ladies. This man will

express his fears and phobias with you because he

is secure in who he is. This man will strive to

fulfill the purpose for which he was born and you

will get a sense of this as the relationship develops.

For it will be his purpose that will keep him

focused and if he tells you that he sees you within

his purpose, then you definitely have a winner.

THE INSIDE SCOOP

Now that you have a general description of what is

behind Curtain's one, two and three, I want to

show how they are all tied together. I want to also

explain how you, with the EVE EFFECT, can play

a role in all of this. It is extremely important to

understand something. The majority of the men

you meet, have never had modeled before them an

example of what they should be as men and how

they should treat women. And even though there

are men who have options and have it together

mentally and spiritually, they did not become that

way over night. In fact, most have progressed

from being a man with no options, to a man with options but with the wrong mentality. Yes some men, move statuses and don't know how to handle the new status. The other point I want to make is that, you as the woman, can play a great role in the man being what he needs to be, but also what he should not be. Which means, you as the woman, can contribute to the progress of a man being mentally and spiritually together. Show him what you value. Let him know that some things are non-negotiable. We need you to 'train' us on how to treat you. I will explain this shortly.

CHAPTER 3 – YOU'D BE SURPRISED TO KNOW

(Misunderstandings and myths about men)

It is amazing how men are misunderstood when it comes to relationships. Often, not all the times, no one is talking to the men about what is on their minds. We are mostly being judged by the actions or activities of the last guy. Thus, comes the notions and myths that all men must be the same way. In this chapter, I will address head on, some misunderstandings and myths about men. Some of it will absolutely surprise you. Now, I kind of like this chapter because I got some of this information from conducting interviews of approximately 100 women of difference ages, stages, races and statuses. The questions ranged from communication to commitment and what these ladies thought concerning these areas. I want to give you some of what they said, but also I want to lay out a general understanding of how we are, think and operate.

MEN AND COMMITMENT

The general belief I received from the women I interviewed, centered on a man's lack of commitment. It was literally 96% of the women I spoke with personally felt that one of their major issues in their dating relationship is that men just want to play around and not be committed to them. They went as far to say that they believe that most men are afraid of commitment. Well I have some interesting news for you ladies. If you think, feel

or believe that men are afraid of commitment, you

are wrong. WE ARE AFRAID OF HOW YOU

PACKAGE COMMITMENT! We are afraid of

needy and desperate behaving women. Now listen

closely, we as men, want to feel 'needed' by you

but we have a problem with you being overly

needy. Remember the principle from earlier that

men's top priority is to please you? So the

question then becomes, how do you reconcile our

need, with your desire for him, to be committed to

you? You show him that being with you will only

get better by committing to you. Let me go

deeper! Think, if you will, for a moment, what he

did to just get your attention. You may have

'played' hard to get. However, you gave him

enough attention to keep him coming back for

more. Check this out….. the moment he decided

he 'had' to talk to you again, see you again or

spend time with you again, 'starts' the

commitment experience for a man. He was

'committed' to getting to know you or just getting

your attention. Trust me, he plotted, planned and

pursued you better than most top agents go after

criminals. Your response to his actions and

activity, is that 'this guy just won't quit!' You

discovered but misunderstood that he was actually

committed from the start. So what happens after

you have given him some real time and attention?

I would like to say that some of you stop using

your EVE EFFECT and started operating out of

impulses. I know you may be wiping sweat from

your brow and thinking that this is way too much

work for a relationship. However, a real man

believes in working for what he gets and it is for

that reason he better appreciates what he works

for. In other words, when he 'commits' to what he

has worked for, his level of appreciation goes up

for that he worked for. Understand this next

statement..... A man will have a greater

appreciation for you when he 'earns' your time,

your attention and your love. For example, you

have to keep him committed to getting your time

by not appearing so desperate to be with him. He

needs to feel that you 'WANT' to spend time with

him but you don't need to. He already knows that

you could be with anyone you want to and when

you make the decision to go out with him, call

him, or do anything with him, he will appreciate you. So that means, always have something on your calendar even if you don't have a calendar! I hope you caught that. I'm not suggesting that you lie, but I am suggesting that if you don't have anything on a certain day, put down the word 'nothing' on that day and do that! In other words, don't always be available to his every whim. His commitment grows as he continues to 'earn' his way for more of your time, attention and love. The problem most women have is that they don't know 'how' to like a man. In other words, many women give up too much too soon because they 'like' spending time with a man. Uh oh, did I just say that? Yes I did, if commitment is what you desire from a man, know 'how' to 'like' us. That means, show interest and be complimentary to him and

convey to him that the more he keeps doing what

he is doing, the more of your time and attention he

will get. All I am saying is that men equate

commitment with 'having earned' something.

Because, hear me good, a man is not willing to

leave what he has put energy and effort into

attaining. He appreciates it so much more than

having things and stuff just handed to him. This is

pretty much true of people. People treat things

they earn better than things that are just given to

them. This is even truer for men and commitment.

You are going to have to change your thinking

about men. It is not the wisest thing to do to give

us things we have not earned to have or keep. But

if your desire is to have him remain committed

from the start of just getting your number to him

wanting to spend the rest of his days with you, he

needs to know that being with you is the best thing

he has ever 'worked' to have.

YOUR LOOKS

Let me give clarity here for millions of women.

Men aren't as shallow as you think. A real man

knows that the most attractive woman in the world

doesn't automatically mean she is relationship

worthy. Sex worthy, yes, but not relationship

worthy. Your looks must come with added

features! For instance, a sense of humor, a level of

'down to earthiness,' a good heart and an ability to

want to know more than she already knows are to

name a few. Somebody say "break that down

Anthony!" For example if you are attractive to him and you are able to joke around without being over the top, it is definitely a major plus with us. We, as men, find it hard being the only one having to come up with funny stuff all the time. However, if the humor is balanced between the two of you, it will add a wonderful foundational component for a life long relationship. It is just that your looks or sexiness alone is not enough to sustain a man's attention. When it comes to you having a good heart, it let us know that you aren't selfish and self centered. Now understand this when I tell you, that if a woman is gorgeous on the outside and yet selfish, he may have sex with her, but she should not expect anything more. Don't get the sex mixed up with anything else other than sex. Lastly when

I speak about you as a woman being diverse, I am

talking about your ability to adapt to most

situations. In other words, if things don't go as

planned, you take the pressure off the man by

being flexible about the situation at times. A

simple, "oh it's ok that things didn't pan out like

you wanted, can you make it up to me?" That, to

us, is the perfect hook to any melody of music in

our ears. However, 'some' women with breath

taking beauty, take on the attitude that 'everything'

has to be perfect, 5 star, and flawless all the time

because they believe their looks deserve it all the

time. Yes, we as men love your beauty, but it does

not trump all other tangible attributes that a women

should have. Because the truth is, we can always

come in contact with someone who may be as

beautiful, if not, more beautiful than you physically. The point here is to note that beauty isn't the final deal maker in our pursuit of having 'THE ONE!'

MEN AND THEIR EMOTIONS

If there was one major misconception made about us as men is that we aren't emotional. Well if you believe that we, as men aren't emotional, you are greatly misinformed. Believe it or not, men are just as emotional as women are. What must be understood is how men manifest their emotions. Ladies, you probably have heard it before and it is worth repeating, we as men, OFTEN express our emotions in a more physical way than any other way. I'm not just speaking sexual intercourse, but rather through acts of kindness and physical affection. The more deep his emotions are, the more of this kind of behavior will increase. Public displays of affection is a great sign of how we feel about you. Now, this is not the RULE but it is a more prevalent behavior from men. Women on the other hand, like more verbal expressions of emotion from men, because that is the way women express themselves. We as men, want more physical displays of emotions because that is the way we are. Therein, lies the problem. We must have a healthy balance of both ways from both sides. However, the emotional display of men can be difficult simply due to the fact of societal expectations. Men have been to 'taught' not to display any emotions. It is the fear of seeming emasculated for many men as to why

they have difficult times expressing their emotions.

I personally feel that if you have a husband or mate

that knows how to express himself emotionally,

verbally and respectfully, you have a blessing.

The old adage of "I can't read your mind," has hurt

many relationships because it leaves room for

assumptions. Ladies, I understand that if your man

doesn't communicate it puts limitations on the

relationship. My question to you is, could you

really handle a man that comes to you with his

feelings, emotions, weaknesses and fears? This is

a major dilemma that we face as men. Can we

really and truly give you all of us without it

coming back to haunt us. To be honest, as a man,

it is not a chance most men are willing to take. We

often would rather, internalize our problems to the point of stress and even death to have to deal with the ridicule of being called or perceived as weaklings. Yet, the myth that we are not emotional is just that.....a myth. We just express our emotions differently. You could really save a man's life by providing him with a place comfortable enough to express himself emotionally. We as men, really need healthy outlets in our lives and it should start with the woman we love, in our lives.

MEN AND THE DOUBLE STANDARD

Ok ladies, if there are one or two chapters in this entire book where men are going to take issue with me, it will definitely be this chapter. Most will not want to admit to you that we have a

'DOUBLE STANDARD' about certain things

when it comes to relationships. In particular, when

it comes to infidelity and extramarital affairs, there

is a double standard. Most guys have the mindset

or belief, that their main chick, 'old lady', wifey or

any other label to describe the woman who comes

'first,' can not under any circumstance do what

they do when it comes to infidelity or an

extramarital affair. Most men, not all, will not

forgive their main woman who cheats or 'messes'

around on them even if the men are having an

affair or fooling around themselves. The way

many men think, it is that it is 'only' sex. Once

again ladies, I'm not talking about right or wrong

here, I'm just talking about reality. Several other

books out there have pointed to this reality as well.

That in the eyes of some men, having something a

little extra on the side, is okay as long as 'home' is

taken care of. Why is this a prevalent mindset you

may ask? It is because 'the main lady'

(wife/girlfriend) is always in place and it can be

predicted that they aren't going anywhere. It's

interesting to note that if at any time she is 'out of

place' when he may be out doing his 'thing,' it is a

problem for him. In other words, some men feel

they can 'check' their woman even if they are out

with another woman. So what's a woman to do?

Well, let me give you a true story about a young

lady who sought my advice once on how to deal

with her husband being out late or even not

coming home at all. Now, what I initially said to

her wasn't easily accepted. But I told her, if you

do what I tell you to, I can almost guarantee, he

won't be out doing anything without your

knowledge or 'permission!' (I will explain that

statement a little later!) So, here's what I said, first

of all, he is cheating or trying to! I asked, do you

believe me? Her reply was, well I guess and 'if' I

catch him, the marriage is over! I said ok, if that's

what you want then, but what do you want at this

point? Do you want him home every night? Do

you want him to stop going out all the time? What

exactly do you want? I asked. Her response was,

"I want him home with me and our children." I

said, ok listen closely and do what I say. I said, in

his mind, you and your family are totally separate

entities in his mind. In his mind, he is not

disrespecting you or the home by being out. He is

paying the bills, he is giving you all family time.

But for whatever reason, he feels he can be with

someone else. You and the home are his comfort

zone and nothing he is doing, is threatening his

'castle.' If he's out and he calls, he knows you

will answer, right? She said "yes, I'm here with

our kids." I said, right but I want you to "double

the double standard." She said, "What?" I said I

want you to flip it on him! She said, "flip it?" I

said yes, flip it! Her initial reply was, "I feel I

shouldn't have to do all of that. Whatever is in the

dark, will come to the light!" I said you are

correct, so let me put the switch in your hand! I

said, write down a few fake phone numbers with

initials on them and strategically place them where

your husband could see them. I said also, get the

best outfit you have (that one neck breaker outfit

you have) and lay it out on the bed around the time

he usually leaves. Now if he asks you about the

numbers, tell them it's just a friend from work,

school, etc…. (You all stay with me!) If he gets

upset, tell him, if you were at home, I'd be talking

to you, but since I am cooped up in this house all

the time, I can at least talk to friends on the phone.

She replied, "I don't know about this." I told her,

once he sees his 'castle' is under threat, he will be

thinking twice about leaving it. I said, now if he

asks you about your 'neck breaking outfit' just say

that you decided to go out, when he goes out. Tell

him you want to go out sometimes yourself since

he is always gone and I have a babysitter who is

going to see about the kids. I told her, now put on

your 'poker face' to let him know you are serious.

You aren't going to argue with him anymore about

his chronic absenteeism at night with his 'friends!'

Tell him you have found some 'friends' yourself!

She reported that her husband not only stop staying

out late, he only wanted to do couples outings with

his wife. She asked me, "How did I know it would

work?" I said, you have to deal with us head on

with things like this. For however long he has

been doing this, is the same amount of time you

have been predictable. You have to switch it up.

If he calls, act like you are too busy to talk to him

because he is obviously where he wants to be. No

man likes for his 'comfort zone' to be under the

possible threat of another man doing to his home,

what he is possibly doing somewhere else when all

he has to do is 'watch' his castle himself. It's a

double standard and when a woman doubles the

double standard, it gets our attention. In our

minds, our 'main lady' can never do what we do.

But you have to let him know that whatever he

does, YOU CAN AND WILL DO BETTER! (even

though you may not)

NOTES:

CHAPTER 4 – USE YOUR P, GET RESULTS

(Traits every woman have to possess and perform)

When developing this chapter, I knew, just like the opening chapter of this book, would raise some eyebrows. That was partly my intentions. My other reason for bringing out somewhat of a controversial title is to change your paradigm on relationships. Having said that, let me restate in a different way what I said in Chapter 1 about men, and that is, your female anatomy will not guarantee anything stable and long lasting when it comes to marriage or relationships. While I stated earlier in the last chapter, looks can only go so far. Why do I raise this point? Because some of you are still wondering, when you look on Facebook,

Twitter, Instagram etc.... how did SHE get HIM? I want to suggest, she put that 'P' on him.

Women, you must come to know that you have been given some inherent traits. It would also be advantageous that you enhance your ability to have a healthy relationship from your life experiences, observing others and researching information like the book you are reading now. Yes, you already possess or have the ability to posses the following qualities or traits that if you perform them, you will get the results you want. Ironically, they all start with the letter 'P.' (smile)

PATIENCE

Women, turn the clock off. So many women have put themselves on time clocks for things that will require other people to make happen. And when it comes to relationships, you must turn the

clock off if you want the best results in that

relationship. You need to take the pressure off

you! I'm not suggesting that you don't have a plan

with a time frame to reach it when it comes to your

personal goals or career, college, fitness and

business. But relationships need two people to

make it work. Therefore, the clock must be turned

off because many times either you may not be

where you need to be or the person you are with or

want to be with may not be to a level they need to

be. So patience is a must. One of my favorite

quotes I love says, "The only thing worse than

waiting, is wishing that you did." If you have

patience, it will payoff. Let me be clear on

something. Patience does not mean you stop being

productive. Patience has been defined as the

capacity to accept delay without getting angry. If

this is true, and it is, it means that a delay does not

mean a complete denial. The reason why the EVE

EFFECT is reduced to a mere phrase with women,

is because they refuse to exercise PATIENCE. I

want you to know that just because your current

situation has not changed, it does not mean it will

not change. If you listen to all success stories, they

will all tell you it didn't happen overnight. It took

some time, it took work. I did not say or will I

ever say that being patient is easy to do. Now, up

until this point, I have not really mention the

reality of God. I was patiently waiting for the right

time and now is that time. I wanted you to trust

me that I knew what I have been talking about. If

you have gotten to his point in this book, that

means you wanted to know more and we have

built some level of trust. So let me say that when

it comes to having patience, it is really a spiritual

attribute that only God can perfect in your life. If

you are married and you need better interaction,

reaction or some action from your husband, your

ability to be patient is imperative. You never, I

repeat, never want to make a permanent decision

for a temporary situation. Patience is the only

thing that will help you do such. Now, of course, I

am not condoning that you take being disrespected

or being endangered, but outside of those things,

you must have patience with your husband. You

must be patient enough to stroke his ego. If you

sense that his ego may be damaged, recall the

things I shared with you previously to help him

recover from having had his ego damaged.

Patience is also needed with men who like

routines. For some of you ladies, this is an okay

behavior. For others, you completely hate

redundancy. However, if that is where your mate

is, patience is needed more than ever. In the next

chapter, I will explain what you can do, to get

better results in this area.

PROVIDE

Well, this should be some enlightening

information for you! When I use the word

provide, I am talking about you 'providing' the

man with some things he 'NEEDS' and often, his

greatest need is to be 'trained' by you. Ok slow

down and don't read into something that I have not

said yet. When I speak of the woman providing

'training' for the man, it means that you are

teaching or training him how to treat you.

Remember that most men that you will meet will

fall into three categories; men with no options,

men with options but the wrong mentality and men

with options who has it together mentally and

spiritually. However, every type of man can be

trained and needs to be trained on how to treat you.

One of the major mistakes we make as men is

treating our new mate like our old one. We often

don't realize that what worked with our last

relationship will not necessarily work in the new

one because you are not the same person. So, we

need to be trained on how to properly treat you.

Listen closely, because much of what you have already learned will come into play now. Remember what was said regarding men's ultimate desire is to please and or turn you on? Well, if he is into you, he will do what ever it takes to get more of your time and attention, but if all he has to go on is what the last woman like and desired and you may be completely different from her, it may be a problem, you think? So, provide him with a new set of rules to your relationship. This is going to require wisdom, confidence and skill. Because some men's focus will be to sleep with you, but what he really needs is to get to know you. With training, you can neutralize his ambitions to sex you and instead see the real you.

There are two ways to be successful in providing the training needed for us men. First of all, set some godly standards for what you need. Secondly, don't compromise the first one. You must have the ability to stand on your standards. When you do and a 'potential' does not meet your godly standards, you don't lose anything that you never had. But let me give you some examples of how to train us. Now understand, for the same reason many women do not care for the word 'submitting' in a relationship, you may get the same reaction from men when they hear the word 'training' when it comes to them and relationships. Because I personally understand the principle, neither word bothers me. But what does bother me is that most women who have yet to get their desired results from a man is that they take the

mindset that they don't have time to 'train' a man

to do anything. Well, that may have been the

problem! You wasted a great deal of time

a'hoping and a'wishing and a'praying for your

mate to get it together. However to him, he felt

like the thing he did in his former relationship

should automatically work with you. When all

you have to do is 'provide' your mate with a

training regimen to help him become the 'perfect'

mate for you! Here's what you do. Get a piece of

paper or type out a list of things you would like for

him be do. On one side you have the 'to do' side

and on the other side you put 'his reward.' When

he does something you like, on the list, respond

with the corresponding reward. Now this is not

manipulating him, for which I will discuss later,
but this is letting him know, 'when you do this, it
makes me do that!' Watch his demeanor and
behavior towards you when it comes to things that
use to drive you crazy because he refused to do. I
found out the biggest area that women complained
about in their relationships were men not helping
with chores. Another was that they have gotten
lazy in the romance department. They also really
chimed in on saying he rarely says 'thank you.'
These are just to name few. Remember, you
possess THE EVE EFFECT, just know what you
want, express it and wait till he does it. When he
does, 'reward' him. Remember, what we earn, we
appreciate!

PURPOSE

A woman with purpose is a woman with power. When you know exactly what your purpose is in life, you will be the best wife or girlfriend a man could ever have. Purpose provides focus. Say that with me again, 'PURPOSE PROVIDES FOCUS!' Staying focus is one of the biggest things that you need to be doing in your life. However, it will be difficult to impossible if you don't know your life's purpose. A purpose filled life will not be deterred or distracted from fulfilling that purpose. So how does your purpose give you the results you need in your relationships. If you are single and dating, whatever your purpose is, you can be productive in fulfilling that purpose while building a life with someone who is connected to your purpose. One of the issues women face is they often choose the kind of mates that are not in line with their purpose. Therefore, they can be detoured because they are no longer driven by their purpose, but they are driven by their feelings. The problem with that is feelings change, purpose doesn't change. I once said on the radio, on one occasion, during an interview that, 'yes, opposites can attract, but it is best to be with someone going in the same direction you are!' I want you to know ladies, whether you are married or single, the quicker you start living life on purpose, your ability to handle your relationship gets better. Because of purpose, you will not engage in activities, arguments, animosity or affiliations that do not line up with your purpose. You possess the greatest combination for success in every area of your life if you capitalize on it. That combinations is that of 'THE EVE EFFECT' and Purpose! Remember, when God created the woman, HE saved the best for last and equipped her with everything she needed to help the man be everything he needs to be. With that being said, when you realize in a more specific way, what your purpose is in life, your love life will have its proper place in that purpose and not have you feeling that it's your only purpose for living. Purpose will defuse desperation. A better rendition for the word desperation in 2014 has been called 'thirsty!' So let me rephrase my last statement. Purpose will diffuse a woman's tendency to be 'thirsty' for a relationship. The reason being is because a 'thirsty' woman will

settle for anything that resembles a relationship.

Women who have been operating out of frustration

will resort to desperation. However, when you are

living out your God given purpose, HE will be the

center and circumference of your life and that in

and of itself is the foundation of where you must

start, before you start adding people to your life.

<u>NOTES</u>

CHAPTER 5 – BE A FACILITATOR, NOT A

MANIPULATOR

(There's actually a thin line you should not cross)

I once read a quote that said, "Women marry men with the hopes of changing them and men marry women with the hopes they won't change!" Wow! Isn't that something? However it is really a true reality for so many women. They go to great lengths to change their mate into what they want him to be and to do. This is a thin line for you women. In all difference to most opinions, women have the ability to facilitate an environment for change, but to manipulate means that you not only can get him to do what you want but you will be doing it with the wrong motives. This would mean that you have to keep on controlling everything in

the relationship and at some point you will want

something different and it could destroy your

ability to have a healthy relationship. This could

also destroys the man's ability to trust 'when' the

relationship is over. The definition of facilitate

simply means to make easy or easier. Once you

are in a relationship, you must be careful that you

don't become manipulative for things you desire.

Manipulation has been deemed a learned behavior.

It has been defined as to manage or influence

skillfully in an unfair manner. For manipulation

has attached to it, a sense of deception with it. As

much as you desire to always have a favorable

outcome in all situations of a relationship,

manipulation is definitely not the way of going

about it to get it. In this chapter, there are a few

practical things you can do to 'facilitate' an

environment for men to do what you desire, but it

would clearly be their decision to transform and

not from the influence of manipulation.

ALLOW FOR UNWINDING

One of the best ways to facilitate the

opportunity for a man to give you what you desire,

is to allow some time to go by once he is home

from work. Studies have shown that it takes a man

at least 45 minutes to unwind from his day. One of

the last things you want to do to a man when he

hits the door from work, is to bombard him with

stuff and situations. This will cause the man to

automatically want to do whatever he has to in

order to get some downtime from work. In

essence, he may lie, agree with you, shut down or

push back when confronted with issues as soon as

he is home. Of course if something is an

emergency and it would require his immediate

assistance, then by all means let him know.

However, if the roof isn't burning, the toilet isn't

flooding or the bank account hasn't been stolen,

then, by all means, be patient and wait. Because, if

a man is stressed out, BOTH of you will suffer.

You will definitely start feeling 'the disconnect'

sooner or later. He will begin to look for ways to

not have to be in your presence. Please note that

because he loves you, his will put up with or

tolerate your initial concern and treat it as such.

But to consistently go after him as soon as he's

home from work, it will sound like 'nagging' in his

mind and it will start the slow process of

accommodating just for 'peace' sake. His eventual

response will be that he will ask for more overtime

at work just to avoid you and not necessarily

working for extra money. He could possibly be

working for extra 'PEACE" or a "PIECE" from

somewhere else. However, because some women

are adamant about having their way, manipulation

becomes their 'seemingly' only option left in

getting what they want from a man.

WHY MANIPULATION IS A "NO NO"

As I stated previously, the heart of

manipulation is deceit. Deceit is simply distorting

the truth for the purpose of misleading. This is a

major issue with some women in relation to their husbands or boyfriends. Depending on the type of man you have in your life and his love for you, he will allow himself to fall prey to every desire you have even if it is under the guise of manipulation. The other thing that is so critical about manipulation is that most often the manipulator has no real idea they are manipulative. And for a person to be deceptive and don't realize it is dangerous. I will explain a little later when men are extremely manipulative when dealing with women. For now, I want to focus on what are some signs of manipulation.

1. *When a person is ALWAYS 'expecting' the other person to give, but don't give back themselves.*

Now this is tricky because if the man you are

with is just a giver by nature and wants to shower

you with all he can offer, some women lack the

wisdom on how to properly receive in their

relationships. That is to say, that reciprocation is

always in order to nullify the possibility of

manipulation being performed. Random,

spontaneous acts of kindness will cause us, as men,

to feel a sense of value from you. This is a major

ego booster, as you have already learned. Your

husband or boyfriend will go to no end to keep you

pleased and satisfied when his ego is being stroked

and he knows that what he does for you is making

you feel proud to be with him. Remember, motive

is the most important than anything else when it

comes to giving and receiving. In Gary

Chapman's book entitled, the Five Love

Languages, he points out that a person's love

language can be identified as Words of

Affirmation, Acts of Service, Receiving Gifts,

Quality Time or Physical Touch. When it comes

to receiving gifts, if it's your love language, don't

manipulate to get what you want. Facilitate an

opportunity to communicate the reality of what

'love languages' are and that yours may be

receiving of gifts. If he knows, you are turned on

or just ecstatic when he gives you something, it is

not manipulation because everyone is on the same

page about the whole issue of him giving to you

and vice versa.

2. Using Comparisons

Some people don't realize they are being manipulative when they start using comparisons between their mate and someone else. When it comes to men, we take issue with this type of behavior. Since, once again, our goal is to please you, we will oblige or accommodate the woman, so that what we do will rise above the rest in hopes it will meet your approval. However, when women start making it about comparisons, men only see it as having to compete. So to have a man feel like he is competing for you, is so much more different than working for your time and attention. If you are married and you are making comparisons, you are treading dangerous territory for a number of reasons. First of all, he could start doing the same to the woman. If a woman's self

esteem is not strong and in tact, this could literally

become the ultimate Achilles heel in the

relationship. The great principle of do unto others

as you would have them do unto you fits nicely

here. Secondly, most women who do this are

probably making unfounded comparisons. The

question has to arise from the man is, HOW DO

YOU KNOW SO MUCH ABOUT THEM. Unless

they can prove that the person they are comparing

their mate to is truth, it is best not to take this

strategy. Lastly, the comparing your mate to

someone else is pretty childish. The proper

response to such behavior is that if they want them

to be like someone else, they need to go be with

someone else. The key here ladies is to never

compare your mate to someone else, but rather let

your mate know that there is no comparison to

him.

3. **Crying**

Now the mother of all manipulative strategies,

this one may be best of all times. There are two

types of people no one likes to see cry. The first is

babies and next will be women. It really has the

greatest impact on people's emotions because we

inherently feel that babies and women are

defenseless, sort of speak. Like you have already

learned that men are as emotional as women and

when his woman cries it goes straight to his

emotions and he has to respond. So many

daughters learn to use this tactic on their fathers

when they are young. However, some never grow

out of this type of behavior. It has been

scientifically proven that our testosterone levels

decrease when we hear or see a woman cry,

according to Neurobiologist, Noam Seobel.

However, if a man realizes that his woman is using

her tears to weaken him, it now becomes a game of

chess. He will completely avoid you or even leave

to not have to deal with your crying. If he finds

that his 'punishment,' which is you crying, does

not fit the 'crime', of what you wanted done, he

may lash out verbally and tell you to quit. Even at

the risk of being insensitive, he may say it or even

build up immunity to your tears and then if that

happens, you are in deep trouble. Why? Because it

ends up sending a cue that now it's ok and justifies

his decision to possibly disrespect the relationship because he now feels disrespected.

<u>NOTES</u>

CHAPTER 6 – *18 SECONDS*

(Are you sure you want to make this compromise?)

It's amazing that I am able to read your minds when you read some of the titles of the chapters in this book. I'm laughing now because once again, this chapter is not really what you think however, you are close. I actually ran this idea about this chapter by a few women and their first response was…. "He has to last longer than 18 seconds to be with me." My response was 'the 18 seconds has nothing to do with him, but it's all about you!' Thus sparks the discussion. What is this 18 seconds business? Well I had to make a decision to either address this subject or ignore it. I decided to address it head on, because I really want to empower women like never before. However, I

must admit that this chapter is a bit controversial.

There is a group of women who have never

experienced the '18 seconds.' There is also a

group of women who always partake of the '18

seconds.' Lastly, there is a group of women

reading this book who live to experience '18

seconds' because they haven't in such a long time.

So I guess it is safe to say that you have picked up

on the contextual clues what '18 seconds' is

dealing with. Yes, it's about sexual intimacy, but

more importantly, a certain aspect of that intimacy.

Well let me go ahead and tell you what the '18

seconds' thingy is and how it relates to men.

First of all, I did some thorough research in this

area after I read an article from a gentleman who

brought to my attention what the '18 second' issue

was all about. Listen to his story as I paraphrase

his article. He stated, I have always been

fascinated with women since the age of 14. My

fascination began after my 'first' experience with a

girl I was head over heels in love with named....

Well that isn't important. However, I would spend

hours upon hours in the library trying to learn

everything I could about girls and women. I read

almost everything there was on the female

anatomy. As I got older and went to college the

intrigue was on a whole different level and I began

to put into practice a great deal of skills I learned

from my research. Ironically enough, I discovered

that if I did certain things a certain way to a

woman, I could help bring her to orgasm. I used

the word 'help' because I understood from my

research and experience that a woman's orgasm

involves her being mentally and physically in tune

with her body and mine. And I learned that the

apex of the sexual experience is her orgasm. I

really didn't know at the time to what level her

mental capacity was attached to this euphoric

moment at that time. However, when I got older I

learned that every woman is different and thus my

techniques must match those differences. And

because I am an avid reader and learner of new

things, I found out that the average minimal

amount of time most women experienced a fully

engaged orgasm was '18 seconds.' And so ladies,

when I ran across this article of information, I had

to check it a little further. Only to discover that it

was absolutely true. Yet, as interesting as it was to find that the '18 seconds' experience is true, I wanted to know how men treat women that they know they can 'help' bring them to orgasm.

My research let me know that when a man KNOWS he can completely satisfy a woman in bed, that he often loses the awe and amazement for the woman and the awe and amazement goes into reverse when it comes to the woman. In other words, the roles often flip. Whereas the woman is smitten by the man and the man can be so confident in himself, that he may become cocky and start treating the woman differently, if he is not serious about her. Why? Scientific research shows that beta-endorphins are release for which decreases pain in the body, oxytocin is also released into that part of the brain that increase

feelings of trust and vasopressin which increases

the feeling of bonding all happens during the "18

seconds" of ecstasy for a woman. In laymen's

terms, ladies you really 'LOSE YOUR DA..

MIND' for 18 seconds due to the experience of an

intense orgasm. And when this happens with a

man who is not your husband, you end up

attaching the '18 seconds' to his existence in your

life. You may not want to admit it, but the power

the orgasm has on a woman's mind goes much

deeper than that for a man. And when all of this

plays out, you must understand, that compromising

your 'sanity' for an 18 second sensation may not

be the brightest decision to make. Here's why....

Men can use sex as a means to control,

manipulate and even take advantage of women in

relationships. If a man is great in bed, he can, if he

isn't morally grounded, use a woman's '18 second'

weakness against her. I realize that many women

won't readily admit to the truth of what an orgasm

does to them because I have heard woman say that

sex is overrated. Well if that is your belief, then I

will admit that this chapter isn't for you because

you are more than likely a virgin or not sexually

active. Both are admirable positions to take and I

clearly respect you for that decision. But for the

rest of you reading this, you know what sex does

to you and you especially know if you are with a

man who is great in bed, giving it to you on

demand, you know that if he was to do to another

woman what he does to you, you may catch a case.

But to take this thought even deeper. I want you to

know that if you are not married and having

incredible sex with a man, there are some major

consequences that are attached to it. First of all, he

is not legally or morally obligated to be faithful to

you. I know you may know that, but hear this

from a man's perspective. If we know we 'got

you,' without the vows and ring, then you are

putting yourself in a major compromising position.

I have seen women 'allow' men to not work, drive

her automobile, spend her money and even live

with her because of the '18 second' sensation. I

have also heard women say there is no way I

would allow a man to not work, drive my

automobile, spend my money or even live with me

because he can 'rock my world.' I have heard

them say, 'I will just get me a B.O.B' (Battery

Operated Boyfriend) before I let that happen to

me. Well that is great for them, I guess. However,

someone is still capitalizing off them experiencing

'18 seconds.' i.e. the toy company.

So, the thing I want you to get from this chapter

is that when it comes to us men, being able to help

bring you to your moment of '18 seconds,' we

know that it will afford us some luxuries that we

would not ordinarily have. Because, it

unknowingly affects you mentally in ways you

may have never known. The '18 second'

experience was only meant to be experienced with

your husband because the biological affect it has

on your mind and it would, at the least, be with

someone who has taken vows to protect you and

provide for you.

CHAPTER 7 – LISTEN, LISTEN, LISTEN

(Did you hear what you think you heard?)

In a previous chapter, I mentioned that when men listen to the woman they love, they do it for the sake of ego boosting. However, they do it in wide general terms. Let me refresh your memory. For example, if you tell a man, "baby you are the most fantastic guy in the world because you are always making sure my car is ok for me to drive each day!" What your mate heard out of all that you said was, "FANTASTIC GUY." However, If you tell a man, 'you are really trifling and can't do anything right.' We often take a few key words out of what you said and internalize a general application to those words. So now, our belief about how you feel about us, is that no matter what

we do, you will not be pleased because chances are

you think we are 'trifling' even though we've done

things prior that you gave a loving declaration of

approval. Let me break that down even further.

Most people remember one negative statement

about themselves even though nine other

statements were positive about them. When it

comes to men, we often listen in general terms as

well as speak or communicate in general terms.

So, there are two words you really need to avoid in

understanding how we think. Those two words are

'never' and 'always' in a negative way towards

your mate. 'Never' and 'always' have destroyed

many relationships because that is what we pick up

when being addressed during a heated discussion.

Listen ladies, that's how we think. It is not a

matter of right or wrong. Think back if you can to

the last argument or disagreement you had with

your husband or boyfriend to see if you recall

using the words 'never' or 'always.' Those two

words either caused him to shut down or get

cranked up. The point and purpose of this chapter

is that most women are often the direct opposite.

While, we as men want to just get to the point of a

conversation, women like the details in the middle.

Well there's nothing wrong with that except men

listen and often speak in direct general terms.

Therefore ladies, you must adjust the way you

listen to us and not just hear us. It is said that one

of the most consistent complaints from men about

women is that women don't listen,

So let me give you some scientific research. It is believed that there are four types of communicators. There is the non-listener. This person is only concerned with what they have to say. Their thoughts are the only ones that really matter. For the most part, they aren't interested in paying attention to what others are saying. Secondly, there is the passive listener. These kinds of listeners acknowledge what you are saying, however they will communicate back in vague replies due to the fact that they may not have caught what you were saying. Next, you have a listener. These individuals hear and get what you saying, however they will, most of the time, retain and reply to that which is most interesting to them. Therefore, if they are into the subject then it's a great opportunity for communication. If they are not into the subject, they will zone in and out but appear interested out of courtesy. The last type of listener is an 'intentional or active listener. These are believed to be the best listeners because they are completely in tune with the speaker and the do it with patience and an open mind. And depending on what type of woman you are and the kind of man you are dealing with, will determined your ability to listen and not just hear them.

A great deal of woman only hear men, but don't listen because many want to change their mate into something that they want him to be. It's not about you changing him but rather it is about 'contributing' to his decision to change. I noted something interesting one day watching a popular talk show that involved four women sitting around

a table having a conversation. It completely blew

my mind that they all began talking at the same

time and they heard each other well. But they had

a tough time listening to what each had to say, so

they kind of calmed down to hear what the other

had to say almost on cue. I realized that many

women have the best ability to hear, but not at

listening at times. One more example, I was asked

to give a woman directions because they did not

have access to a GPS device or an ink pen and

paper. And the first thing out of her mouth was,

"I'm not good with directions." In my mind I was

like, well you are in trouble because of where you

need to get to and all you have to do is listen my

directions. If you asked men, whether it is your

father, brother, co-workers and friends what are

some of the things that really gets under your skin

concerning women? You will get in the top five

things is that 'woman don't listen.' Hey while I

got your attention, if I were to ask women what is

one of the things that gets under their skins, they

would have in the top five, 'men don't listen.' The

truth is, they are both correct. The difference is

how! Men will, sometimes, nod yes and give

gestures of agreement just so the woman could

hurry up and be quiet. Why? We aren't always

interested in the fine details just the most important

details. As a result, we want you to be the same

way we are therefore we communicate that with

you. So since this book is about women being

equipped on how to get the results they desire from

men, I must take one side of this perspective to empower the women. Let me explain.

Have you ever found yourself saying to your husband or boyfriend, I know you said that, but why didn't you tell me this? Well he more than likely felt that he told you all the major details and left out the 'minor' ones. The issue with this is that you ended up making decisions based up what you "thought you heard." Unfortunately, he may get upset because you may have did something he thought he told you not to do! We aren't talking about who is right or wrong, but rather how things are in many instances. Now one of the best ways to handle situations that arrive from a lack of complete understanding and communication is to take the time and have enough patience to understand that your husband or mate, may have

left out details that you really needed. What

happens at times when there seems to be a

breakdown in communication, women will often

make a decision based on limited information and

men do the same based upon 'the major'

information. Ladies, it is imperative that you take

time to make sure you get all the pertinent

information about things before you act or react.

So when we talk about listen, listen, listen, I'm

speaking more so of you really taking the time to

make sure you get the correct information before

preceding to do something. Also it is imperative

that you really brush up on your listening skill

because there are some things that men

communicate in a non-verbal way. There is a

quote floating around in our present culture that

says, "When people show you who they are,

believe them." I agree. I have sat across my desk

from women who claimed, "I didn't see the signs."

Often my reply would be, 'He told you, but you

probably wasn't listening.' I think ladies, that of all

the things I have presented to you in this book, this

principle is one of the most important. See, you

are blessed if you have husband or boyfriend who

expresses himself about everything that may be on

his mind. You should not take it for granted if you

have a mate that actually understands the

importance of clear communication. However, you

don't want to be like the women that come to me

for pastoral advice about their mates. They all say

the same thing. He won't talk to me. Understand

that when a man is not talking they are still

communicating with you, however the question is

are you listening? I often ask women what was the

last thing you recall him saying to you? Many

times, I help break down to these ladies that your

greatest clue is the last thing he said. Men often do

not like to repeat conversations over and over

again unless they are in serious trouble with you.

One of the things many woman have to keep in

mind is, if your husband or mate is saying the

same thing and you are raising your voice or re-

phrasing the question because YOU AREN'T

HEARING THE ANSWER YOU WANT TO

HEAR. He may completely shut down verbally

and communicate with you without using words.

Of course there are exceptions to the rule and you

could have a combative mate who wants to and has

to have the last word.

It is important to know how to deal with your

mate when or if he shuts down. The solution is

simple, leave him alone and corner him in such a

way so he has to talk to you. You corner him by

disarming him once he lays down to rest. Just

politely put your head on his chest and tell him, I

really didn't understand what you were trying to

say at the time you spoke before. I really don't

want us not talking to each other, (rub on him

gently while you are talking) and I'm almost

certain he will revisit the conversation without

feeling threatened and reconciliation is possible. If

he still won't talk, depending on the severity of the

situation, 'give it a rest' for now. Remember you

have the EVE EFFECT. I must encourage you

again ladies to not make your home, more

specifically, your bedroom a war zone.

Understand that men like peaceful places to relax.

So, ladies remember these two words, 'pillow

talk!' When our heads are resting on a pillow and

our defenses are down, have the discussion you

desire. You are not being manipulative at this

point, you are just taking advantage of an

opportunity that you both get to enjoy. It is called

intimate quality time.

NOTES:

CHAPTER 8 – PLEASE DON'T....
(Things you may not want to do)

When it comes to you having THE EVE

EFFECT, it is very well possible to lose your

ability to function as you should if you give up the

influence, the persuasiveness, the charisma and

"power" by engaging in activities and behaviors

that work against you and not for you. I want to

take this time to share with you some specific do's

and don'ts when dealing with men. Remember for

the rest of your life that men think differently than

women. To make this easy for you, I will give you

several scenarios that you may or may not be

familiar with, however it's important that you take

heed to the advice I am sharing with you. I will hit

you with the most prevalent ones and then the

subtle ones.

PICTURES

Don't take pictures of yourself from inside

hotel rooms and then post them online. Men think

differently and sometimes we think if you are

always in a hotel room, you like going there!

HINT HINT! Be extremely careful with the

"infamous" side or booty shots. Yes, we all know

you got it! Yes, it is your body and you can do

what you will with it. Yes, you are proud of the

fact that you have lost weight and you are no

longer ashamed of how you look now. But, we as

men, often can care less about the story behind the

glory. All we see is that bootay!! And if you

don't want the conversation surrounding your

looks or taking you to your seemingly favorite

spot, i.e. the hotel, minimize if all possible certain

pictures for view. Don't put it out there. The

shocking response, however, is that a lot of women

get upset because men have a hard time changing

the subject about your figure when it was a major

point of emphasis on pictures. I know it seems this

should not be something to address, but you have

to know how men think.

DATING SITES

We know that the dating scene has changed

enormously in the past twenty years with the use

of the internet at our disposal. There are all kinds

of sites for almost anything that a person is in to. I

want to caution you ladies to not put too much

information on your profile pages. I know you

think that you are eliminating a vast amount of

men who are only wanting to "play games." But

really this is not the best way to accomplish that.

Yes, some men aren't going to take the time and

read what you wrote about your likes, dislikes,

hobbies, etc. And if you give them an opportunity

to talk with you, they may reveal they didn't read

your entire profile because of the redundant

questions they ask because of their lack of

"preparedness" to converse with you. You really

don't want to reveal too much because, there are a

great number of men who will read it all, prepare

themselves, reach out to you and say exactly what

you want to hear. For example, a lot of women

will put "religious" or "spiritual" information and

think that will deter the kind of guy they don't

want. However, men have figured out, that if they

can talk the talk, they can keep the conversation

going. My point is this, only give simple, short

statements when doing an online profile. They're

a great deal of men who could care less that you

like to do some of the things that you do based on

an online profile especially if he finds you

flawlessly beautiful. Some men see that as an

open book test. Even more so, you want to leave

room for the conversations that may take place.

Something else you must consider when going on

online dating sites and that is don't believe

everything you read. Here's a little trick some

men could play on you. They can read numerous

amounts of women's profiles and then tailor their

profile to fit what most women want especially

when the objective is to get a date with you. Some

women fall for the "his profile says," and that does

not qualify for reasons to completely give yourself

over to what you read. Remember, people can be

who ever they want to be online. The extremely

popular MTV reality show "Catfish" has proven

this point many times over.

DATES

Okay its time to really educate you on what not

to do on dates with someone you just met. The

reason I am addressing the initial dating stage is

because if the man can get past this stage with you,

you can know what to expect on later dates. I want

to give some privileged information here. First

thing, do not allow a man to pick you up at your

house nor you pick him up at his house during the

initial dating stage. Under no circumstances

should you do this. Always meet him at the place

you are going to. Why you say? The most

important reason is because you don't know them.

For your safety, you should meet him at the

location of the date and you should do your due

diligence of the location. Far too often, women let

their guard down too easily in the beginning of

dating someone all because you "feel" he is

okay.(I will share with you when to "feel") The

other reason you want to meet him at the date

location is because you get to see how he

"performs." In other words, you get to see if he is

prompt. You get to see if he put some thought into

where you meet by making reservations if

necessary and when he is meeting you. Be careful

of late night dates initially.

Now that you are at the place, watch how he

handles himself. Pay attention to see that you have

his undivided attention. Watch his eyes! Watch

your eyes too! Make sure that you two aren't more

engaged with your cell phone than each other. If

you have children and you have to periodically

check your phone, let that be known up front.

Otherwise don't even pull the cell phone out.

Additionally, try to not be out past midnight on

the first 4 to 5 dates especially if you have

consumed alcohol during the date. When you

combine alcohol and a weary body, it is possible

you will drop your guard down and begin to open

yourself up to conversations and "activities" that you would not normally do with strangers. Dates are designed for the man to "court" you, which means to pay special attention to someone in an attempt to "win" their favor. So many woman take on the role of the person doing the courting and that can become a problem. I want to deal with something else on dates you must consider and that is your date's manners towards you and your server. If your date is rough and abrasive when dealing with your server or host at the place you are patronizing, that should throw up a red flag. In more particular, watch what they give as a tip for the service you have been rendered. Now of course, if the service was horrible, then you can use your discretion. However, if the service was excellent, find out what he is giving as a tip. Now

if you are a horrible tipper yourself, you will see

no value in what I am about to say. Because if a

person has been given great service and they don't

appreciate it through the tip, then most often they

could be completely self centered. However the

opposite could also be true. That when the man is

a great tipper he may have a generous heart and

understands the importance of appreciating people

doing things for him. This should be a big plus for

him and a relief to you.

ASSUMPTIONS

Let me say that one, if not the biggest mistakes,

I have made in my all my years of ministry and

pastoring, is assuming. One of the biggest, if not

the biggest, mistakes I have made in relationships

is assuming. What does assumption mean? It

means to accept something to be true without

proof. I know that while you are reading this, your

mind is going back through your life experiences

and you are reminded of the reality that most of the

issues and situations you faced could have been

avoided had you not made certain assumptions.

You don't want to make assumptions a regular part

of how you operate in relationships. Seek clarity

where you don't understand or something doesn't

make sense. You have to be responsible enough to

ask questions. If it seems tedious or even time

consuming, it is best to ask the tough questions to

get clarity than to assume and end up heartbroken

and alone as a result. Now sometimes, some men

aren't going to want to deal with the tough

questions when it pertains to them. So even the

playing field with him by letting him know that

one of the parameters of your relationship that you

don't want to make assumptions about each other

and that if it's something he wants or needs to

know, then ask. As well as, the same is true for

you. That is, if you want to know something, you

have the green light to ask. Why is this so

important? We cannot read each other's minds.

Yes, we may know things about each other and can

predict certain actions. That isn't what I am

addressing here. I'm addressing those gray areas.

Where you find yourself, asking yourself, that

doesn't make sense. The reason some people

would rather make the assumption on things rather

than get clarity is because they do not want to

appear "not having it together." At the risk of

embarrassment, it is to your advantage to ask and

not assume. Men can be really good at using your

assuming to their advantage. It is nothing for some

men to say, "You didn't ask." So remember you

have the EVE EFFECT. You have been

empowered on how get a man to open up to you.

Use your power and ask when you aren't sure.

Because one of the worst things you can ever do is

to be head over heels in love with a liar. To

continually assume things about your mate because

you 'love' them is really dangerous. Therefore if

you find yourself with a liar, know that you cannot

do, say or hope enough for them to change. You

must realize that their lying has nothing to do with

you but everything to do with them. You MUST

be willing to walk away. Yes, people can change,

but change is never controlled by exterior stimuli.

Change only takes place when a person's inner

being is transformed. Ladies, I must admit without

bad mouthing my male counterparts, we can, if we

aren't spiritually grounded, can take a lie with us

to the grave. Often, we are able because the

women we are with assume they have us figured

out and we are always predictable. That's not

always the truth. We, as men, must have a great

deal of accountability along with being responsible

for our actions. So, if you have a 'hunch,' a

'feeling,' a 'notion,' or 'intuition,' don't assume,

just ask. It could save you time and even your life.

AN EXTRA SIDE NOTE

As a man, telling you about men, I am not interested in bashing men. This is not the purpose of this book. This book is more about men being able to become better men because of the value and influence you have on us. It is my firm belief that a man can only reach his full potential when he has an "EVE" in his life. However, I am well aware, that SOME men have no clue as to the value and importance the woman's place is in relationships. So, as an extra side note, I want to say that under no circumstances should you negotiate your life, your time and your love for a man that is an abuser. If a man loves, honors and respect you, he will never, under any circumstances, verbally or physically abuse you.

You must be smart enough, woman enough and willing to end the relationship the moment it happens. If a man will not verbally or physically abuse his mother, then he should not do it to you. Ironically enough, there are some men who have not one ounce of respect for their mother or women in general and so if you end up in a relationship with this kind of man, be willing to get out the relationship and encourage him to get professional counseling. Because, if you understand what has already been spoken in chapter one dealing with The Ego, you know the first ego stroker and builder is a man's mother. Therefore, there are some internal issues that must be handled before a man that is disrespectful to his mother, can be in a relationship with a woman like you.

<u>NOTES</u>

CHAPTER 9 – YOUR SECRET WEAPON

(I saved the best for last...you can thank me later)

When thinking through my years of interacting with women both on the levels of professional, friendship or relationships, I noticed something very interesting on how they related to me and other men. I notice that the women who had a strong, vibrant and loving relationship with their fathers, were different from those who didn't. In addition to that, I noticed also that those women who had strong, vibrant and loving relationships with male siblings were different than those who didn't. Now of course there were exceptions to the rules but those women who had a great deal of male influence in their lives were not easily swayed by lines, lies or looks. The ones who did not have those influences often fell prey to lines, lies and looks because they often just desired attention from a man and because they were not trained to protect themselves they often became victims to the circumstances.

I would like to introduce to you somewhat of a new concept that will help strengthen the "effect" you can have on men and put you at an advantage of knowing how men think so you can respond to us in a way that is productive to your relationships. I'd like to call it your "secret" weapon. I know most men are going to be upset that I'm arming you with this, but I realize so many women need help in the area of healthy relationships. In addition, since we, as men, come to you thinking we "want" one thing, when actually it's something

else we "need" altogether different. Many times

we don't realize it until that one woman, who

understands her worth, her value, her "EVE

EFFECT" that we will adjust our attitudes and then

our actions will follow. So what is this secret

weapon? Well I must tell you that through much

research and reflection, the results were that every

woman needs a "MALE MENTOR!" Think about

that for a moment. Listen to how that sounds.

Well the first thing you must consider is, what is a

mentor? A mentor is defined as "an experienced

and trusted advisor." So there you have it! Your

secret weapon is to have an experienced and

trained male advisor.

WHO QUALIFIES AS A MALE MENTOR

Many women feel as though they have

someone to go to ask questions about their

relationships with men. The irony is that

"someone" is usually another woman. I'm not

against this idea. I just know you will be limited in

all you could know. Then, there are a few women

who have figured out one of their best resources is

a man when talking about their relationship.

However, most only take some things to those men

for advice but not everything. The reason being is

that a great number of women have a great level of

independence that permeates their decisions when

it comes to dealing with men. It often leads to

bewilderment and heartbreak because they

overestimated their own ability to understand men.

The second reason women only share some things

and not everything for advice, is because they feel

that they can not trust that particular advisor with

that kind of information under no circumstances.

Well, therein lies the problem. I will readily admit

to you that you are right. You can not share

everything with someone of the opposite sex

except with a "MALE MENTOR." This person

isn't just anyone. He will be your "experienced

and trained adviser." He must have the following

qualifications:

1. *HE CAN NOT BE SOMEONE YOU COULD*

DATE OR HAVE A RELATIONSHIP WITH.

As you can see, that eliminates a great deal of men.

So with that being said, your male mentor should

be your father, your sibling, cousin, your uncle or

even a nephew. Ideally, your male mentor should

be a relative. There are exceptions to that, but I

am not advising you to go outside that pool for a

Male Mentor. **2.** *YOU HAVE TO KNOW THEIR*

VIEWS ON WOMEN AS A WHOLE AND OF

YOU! This is going to require some humility and

creativity on your part. You will need to initially

interview your MALE MENTOR without him

knowing he is being interviewed. Now if you are

saying to yourself you aren't going to go through

all of this trouble for a relationship, then by all

means don't. However, check your track record.

Be honest, if you could have known some things

upfront about your ex or your current, you would

have made some different choices. Well, here's

your opportunity! I suggest you get any and every

question you've ever wanted to ask a man and set

aside some time with your potential "Male

Mentor" to interview them. You need to know

how your potential Male Mentor interacts, views

and treat women. This is for your own comfort

level. However, you don't want to stop with their

view of other women, you need to know how they

see you. You may be surprised to find out how

they really feel about you. Because what you may

find out is that they see you differently from

"other" women and they may view you no

different than other women. In either scenario,

you need to know these things. You must be

patient and willing to stay the course to choose the

right 'secret weapon!'

3. *I WOULD SUGGEST THAT YOUR MALE MENTOR IS SPIRITUALLY SOUND!* This is probably one of the most important characteristics your mentor should have. Because you will need a great deal of balanced advice. You need someone who will give you "the real" 411 from a man's natural point of view but also you will need to hear advice from a supernatural point of view. In other words your male mentor must be a praying man. You will need someone who will walk along side you and give some spiritual guidance when you go through the most difficult times. Now, I realize that everybody can't fit that role, but it is going to be necessary for your peace and happiness in relationships.

ONCE YOU HAVE YOUR MALE MENTOR

Now I want to give you some specific things

you must know once you have "an experienced

and trusted male adviser." You have to be able to

be comfortable with bringing any subject or any

situation to your MALE MENTOR no matter how

sensitive or embarrassing it may seem. YOU

MUST BE WILLING TO PUT IT ALL ON THE

TABLE. It must be clearly understood that if there

is one subject that all men know about is men. We

know every trick, gimmick, scheme, plot, ploy,

game, line, lie, intention, motive, meaning and

mentality of men. So you must really change your

mindset on how you will approach relationships

from now on. You can go at it alone, or have

"inside" help. I have been a male mentor for

several years to a couple of my female relatives. I

qualify to be their mentor for several reasons.

One, yes I am a Pastor, but secondly I have had a

great deal of experience with women in my life.

They know this and they completely trust my

advice. It is sad to say that they have not always

brought things to me for help because they were

either too embarrassed or because they thought

they could "handle" the situation. Needless to say,

they now understand the importance of having me

in their lives under this role. I definitely want the

best for them and I would never want them taken

advantage of by men who mean them no good!

They have given me numerous of testimonies of

how the things that I have said happened almost on

cue. But for you who are reading this book, you

may not have a male mentor with all the

qualifications, but one qualifying fact must be true

and that is he can't be in a position to ever have a

relationship with you. I do understand that being

open and honest with someone outside your

relationship my may seem a bit too much, but you

must seriously give it some thought. For some

who have read this book and the others who

haven't, must know, that if you want some things

you have never had before, you have to do some

things you have never done before!

THE BEGINNING

Most books conclude with the final two words,

THE END! Well not so with this book. I would

like for you to leave knowing that it this is now the

beginning for you in your quest to be in a healthy

and long lasting relationship. We are not and will

never be perfect human beings, yet we can be in

relationships that are perfect for us. With that in

mind, you can have everything God says you can

have, you can do what HE says you can do and

you are who HE says you are, which is "fearfully

and wonderfully made!" I will be praying for your

marriage, your relationship and your family! You

have been given the power of THE EVE EFFECT.

Use it wisely! Thank You!

Made in the USA
Charleston, SC
28 February 2015